DEC – – 2010

THE *Missing* SHOP MANUAL

DRILLS *and*
DRILL PRESSES

{ the tool information you need at your fingertips }

skills institute
press

Distributed By
Fox Chapel Publishing

FOX CHAPEL
PUBLISHING

Drills and Drill Presses is an original work, first published in 2010.

Portions of text and art previously published by and reproduced under license with Direct Holdings Americas Inc.

ISBN 978-1-56523-472-7

Library of Congress Cataloging-in-Publication Data

Drill and drill presses.

    p. cm. -- (The missing shop manual)

Includes index.

ISBN 978-1-56523-472-7

1. Drill Presses. 2. Electric drills. I. Fox Chapel Publishing
TJ1263.D75 2009
621.9'52--dc22

                    2009036162

To learn more about the other great books from Fox Chapel Publishing,
or to find a retailer near you, call toll-free 800-457-9112
or visit us at *www.FoxChapelPublishing.com*.

Note to Authors: We are always looking for talented authors to write new books
in our area of woodworking, design, and related crafts.
Please send a brief letter describing your idea to Acquisition Editor,
1970 Broad Street, East Petersburg, PA 17520.

Printed in China
First printing: February 2010

Contents

WHAT YOU WILL LEARN

Chapter 1
Choosing a Drill, page 6

Chapter 2
Drill Bits, page 10

Chapter 3
Drilling Basics, page 14

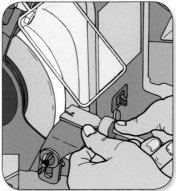

Chapter 4
Sharpening Drill Bits, page 24

Chapter 5
Drill Joinery, page 36

Chapter 6
Repair and Renovation, page 46

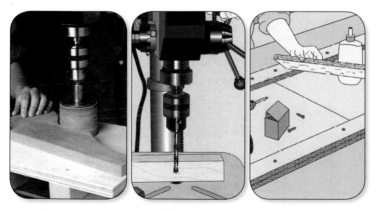

Chapter 7
Drill Press,
page 52

Chapter 8
*Drill Press
Operations,*
page 64

Chapter 9
Cabinetmaking,
page 84

CHAPTER 1

Choosing a Drill

Although all electric drills operate in essentially the same way, woodworkers often keep several different models on hand to take care of any drilling operation. For most applications, a 12 volt or 14.4 volt cordless ⅜-inch variable speed, reversible drill is ideal.

Early cordless models often sacrificed power for portability, but more recent versions have solved this problem and can produce more than enough torque for all drilling jobs. A common feature is an adjustable slip-clutch mechanism. When driving screws the clutch allows the bit to spin only as fast as the screw turns; when the screw stops rotating so too does the bit. This prevents the bit from stripping the screw head or slipping off the screw and marring the workpiece.

Another feature you should look for is a reversing switch for removing screws or withdrawing a bit that is stuck in a hole.

CORDED AND CORDLESS

While cordless drills have become very popular in recent years, there's still a place for a corded drill in the tool kit. If you are an occasional woodworker or home handy-person, who doesn't use a drill from one month to the next, the moment you need your cordless unit you're liable to find its battery depleted. You might conclude that you are better off with a corded drill that's always ready to go.

The same could be true if you are a very active woodworker. For example, when assembling a large and complex project, you may need to drill hundreds of holes and drive dozens of screws. You would be slowed down by having to stop and re-charge a cordless drill.

In either situation, perhaps the best solution is to have two drills: one corded, the other cordless. You will find many situations when it's very handy to have both – a bit for boring pilot holes in one, a tip for driving screws in the other.

ANATOMY OF A CORDED DRILL

Motor bearing Located at end of motor shaft to reduce friction as motor armature spins; may be sealed

Brush assembly A spring-loaded carbon rod encased in a housing; conducts current to the motor armature. Sparks flying from the motor is a sign of worn brushes.

Chuck

Chuck jaws Hold and rotate bit

Reversing Switch Changes direction of motor rotation

Variable speed trigger switch Dials sets motor speed

Power cord

ANATOMY OF A CORDLESS DRILL

Quick-Change Chuck

Torque Adjustment

Speed Range Switch

Chuck jaws
Hold and rotate bit

Reversing Switch
Changes direction of
motor rotation

Variable speed trigger switch

Battery Release

Rechargeable Battery Pack

CHAPTER 2

Drill Bits

Your electric drill's versatility is limited only by the range of bits you accumulate.

As shown here, a wide array of these implements is available, from twist and brad-point bits for boring holes of different diameters and depths to counterbore bits for drilling recessed screw holes.

The popular twist bit bores holes from $\frac{1}{32}$ to $\frac{1}{2}$ inch in diameter. Originally designed for drilling into metal, twist bits tend to skate on a surface before penetrating. Improve performance by punching a starting hole with an awl before boring.

Most woodworkers prefer brad-point bits. Available with carbon steel, high-speed steel, or carbide-tipped cutting edges, the sharpened centerpoint of a brad-point bit allows accurate positioning. Better-quality bits feature two spurs on the perimeter that score the circumference of the hole before the chipping bevels clear away the stock. Twist bits are a better choice for angled holes.

Drill bits are virtually maintenance-free but will only work properly if they are kept sharp.

Stop collar
Also called drill stop or depth gauge; for drilling to an exact depth. Available in sets matching bit diameters, typically from $\frac{1}{8}$ to $\frac{1}{2}$ inch. Hex wrench supplied for installing on bit.

DRILL BITS

Twist bit

The least expensive of commonly used drill bits; flutes expel wood chips during drilling. Sold singly or as sets.

Brad-point bit

Produces smooth, precise holes from ⅛ to ¾ inch in diameter. Features a sharpened centerpoint to guide bit and two spurs which score the circumference of the hole before the chipping bevels begin removing stock

Spade bit

Bores large holes up to 1½ inches in diameter; sharp centerpoint guides bit while flat blade slices into stock. Some bits have spurs on shoulders for cleaner holes.

Extractor bit

For removing screws with stripped heads; features reverse threads.

Multispur bit

Also known as sawtooth bit; bores clean, smooth, nearly flat-bottomed holes. Rim does not heat up as quickly as Forstner bit.

Forstner bit

Bores perfectly flat-bottomed holes. Razor rim guides bit while chippers cut.

Screwdriver bit

For driving slotted, Phillips or Robertson screws of various diameters.

Counterbore bit

Adjustable combination bit that simultaneously bores pilot hole, screw shank clearance hole, countersinking hole and counterbore hole for screws.

Fly cutter

Also known as a circle cutter. Cuts holes from 1½ to 8 inches in diameter. Cutter blade is adjusted for different diameters by loosening a setscrew and sliding the cutter blade in or out.

DRILL ACCESSORIES

Plug cutter

Cuts wood plugs up to ½-inch long to conceal counterbored screws; chamfers one end of plug for easy installation.

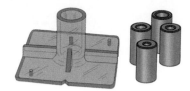

Drill guide

For keeping drill at fixed angle to flat or round stock. Bushings accommodate various bit diameters.

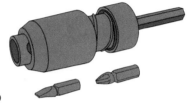

Right-angle head

For working in tight corners; allows accessory in chuck to operate at 90° angle to body of drill. Installed between chuck and drill body.

Clutch adapter

Drives screws without having to drill pilot holes; holds screw securely until head is flush with surface, then clutch disengages to avoid stripping screw head.

Bit sharpener

Hones dull bits; has grinding wheels and chuck to hold bits.

Flap sander

For sanding curved or contoured surfaces; features aluminum head which spins sanding strips.

QUICK-CHANGE CHUCK

One click in and one click out. These chucks make bit changing a snap.

The quick change chuck is a simple device that fits into any drill and costs less than $15. It lets you swap any hex-shank bit or driver in seconds. The chuck's barrel automatically snaps into position, locking the bit in place. To remove the bit, just pull the barrel forward to the unlocked position. It clicks into place, and the bit is loose.

Any bit or driver with a ¼-inch hex shank can fit into a quick-change chuck, including twist bits, spade bits, countersink combination bits, self-centering bits, magnetic tip holders, and nut drivers. Twist bits come in two different styles. In the one-piece bit, the shank is hex-shaped rather than round. A fancier type involves a regular round-shank drill bit fittings into a router-like collet that has a hex shank. If you break or dull a bit, you stick a new one in a collet.

Boring a hole into a piece of wood may seem like a simple task. But when you consider that some wood species are harder to penetrate than others, and that holes for woodworking projects sometimes need to be drilled at precise angles and to exact depths, it becomes clear that this deceptively easy operation holds the potential for error. Precision is as important in drilling as in any other phase of a project. A dowel hole that is off-center or too deep, or a pocket hole drilled at the wrong angle, can mar a project as badly as an inaccurate saw cut or a poorly applied finish. For most operations, accuracy begins with the proper setup. While you can depend on a steady hand to bore a perfectly straight hole, there are a wide variety of commercial guides to help you.

A couple of simple shopmade jigs shown in this chapter make it easy to drill both straight and angled holes.

If you are using a twist bit, punch a starting hole for the bit with an awl. To prevent splintering as the bit exits from a workpiece, clamp a support board between the stock and the work surface. For best results, begin a hole slowly, then gradually increase the speed as you drill. Control the depth of a hole by installing a commercial stop collar on the bit or using the shopmade alternative.

STRAIGHT AND SQUARE

A try square or a shopmade block will help you keep a drill bit perpendicular to a workpiece when you bore a hole. To use the square, line up its handle with the mark for the hole, with the blade pointing up. Centering the bit over the mark, align it with the blade and bore the hole (left). Be sure to keep the bit parallel to the square throughout the operation. To make the guide block, cut a 90° angle wedge out of one corner of a board. Center the bit over the mark, then butt the notched corner of the guide block against it. Clamp the block in place. Keeping the bit flush against the corner of the block (right), bore the hole.

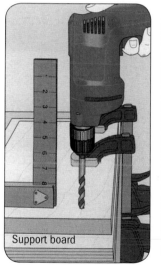

Support board

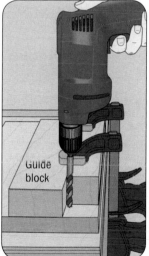

Guide block

ANGLED HOLE

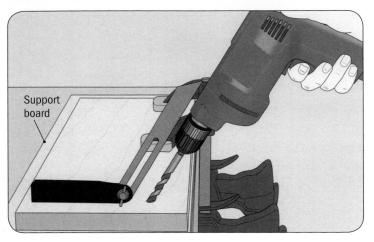

Support
board

Set a sliding bevel to the appropriate angle, then line up its handle beside
the point where you need the hole. Center the bit over the mark, then bore
the hole (above), keeping the bit parallel to the blade while you drill.

*Shop*Tip

Guide block for angled holes

To make a guide block for drilling into
a workpiece at an angle, bore at a
90°angle through a small wood block
with the same bit you will be using for
the angled hole. Then make a miter cut
at one end of the block trimming the
wood at the same angle as the hole
you will be drilling. Cut a notch in one
side of the block to facilitate clamping,
and make a V-shaped notch at the
bottom to help you pinpoint the tip of
the bit. Clamp the block in place when
using it to bore a hole.

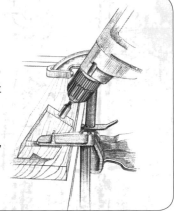

WIDE AND DEEP HOLES

Wide Hole

Drill holes up to 1½ inches in diameter with a spade bit; for wider holes, use a hole saw. In either case, punch a starting hole in the workpiece with an awl. Center the pilot bit over the starting point, and holding the drill with both hands, start drilling slowly. Increase the speed gradually, feeding with only enough pressure to keep the bit cutting into the wood.

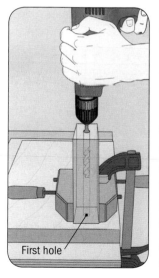

First hole

Deep Hole

To bore a hole that is deeper than your bit is long, make intersecting holes from opposite ends of the workpiece. Begin by punching starting holes at the same point on both ends of the stock. Then secure the workpiece in a handscrew and clamp it to a work surface with one of the starting points facing up. Centering the bit over the mark, bore a hole slightly more than halfway through the stock. Flip the workpiece over and clamp it in position. Center the bit over the other starting point and complete the drilling operation.

ENLARGING A HOLE

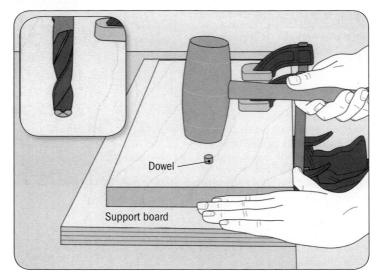

Dowel

Support board

To widen a hole that has already been bored by a brad-point or a spade bit, you will need a solid surface to brace the centerpoint of the bit against. First plug the hole by tapping a dowel into it. Use a dowel the same diameter as the hole for a snug fit and make sure that it is flush with the surface of the workpiece. Mark the center of the dowel, then install the appropriate bit in the drill and bore the wider hole (inset).

HOLES TEMPLATE

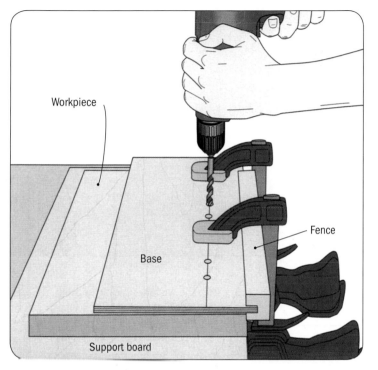

To bore a row of equally spaced holes, use a hole-drilling template made in the shop from ¼-inch plywood. The dimensions of the jig will depend on the size of your workpiece.

To make the template, mark a line on the plywood to align the holes, then drill at the spacing you require. Cut a piece of 1-by-1 stock to the same length as the base and rout a ½-inch-deep, ¼-inch-wide groove along one edge. Glue the 1-by-1 to the base to serve as a fence.

Set your workpiece on a support board, then clamp the template to the stock with the fence flush against its edge. Use the holes in the template to guide the bit into the workpiece.

DRIVING SCREWS

Driving a screw into hardwood without predrilling the hole risks splitting the workpiece or breaking off the head of the screw. Depending on how deeply you need to sink the screw, you may have to bore up to four overlapping holes of different diameters, one inside the next. If you want the screw head to sit on the surface of the wood, bore a pilot hole for the threads and a clearance hole for the shank. For the best grip, a pilot hole should be slightly smaller than the threads of the screw. To set the head flush with the surface, bore a countersinking hole. If you wish to conceal the screw under a wood plug, add a counterbore hole.

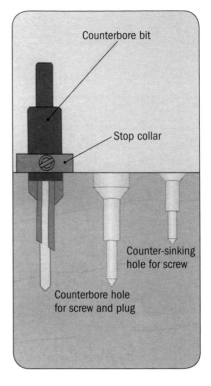

Counterbore bit

Stop collar

Counter-sinking hole for screw

Counterbore hole for screw and plug

There are two ways to bore holes for screws. You can use a different bit for each hole or, as shown here, bore them simultaneously with a counterbore bit.

DRIVING SCREWS *(continued)*

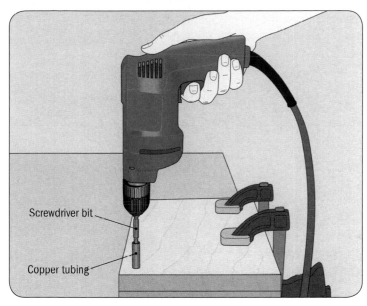

Screwdriver bit

Copper tubing

To screw two pieces of stock together, fit your drill with a counterbore bit of a size appropriate to the size of your hardware. Such a bit will bore a pilot hole and has a stop collar that slides up and down to adjust it for making either counterbore or countersinking holes. Clamp the workpieces one atop the other on a work surface, then bore the hole. If you will be using a screwdriver to install the screw, coat the threads with candle wax to make the fastener easier to drive. To use the drill, install a screwdriver bit and set the screw in the hole by hand. For a slotted head screw, slip a short length of copper tubing around it to prevent the bit from slipping off the head and marring the stock. Fit the bit into the screw head and apply light pressure as you slowly start the drill; gradually increase the feed pressure and drill speed as the screw takes hold.

DRILLING SAFETY TIPS

- Always wear safety glasses when operating a drill; also put on a dust mask if you are using a sanding or scraping accessory.

- Do not use the drill if any of its parts are loose or damaged; inspect your drill bits and accessories before drilling.

- Keep all cords clear of the cutting area.

- Disconnect the drill from its power source before changing a bit or accessory, or making any other adjustments to the tool.

- Keep your hands away from the underside of a workpiece when the bit is cutting into it.

- When installing a bit, make sure you insert it fully into the chuck.

- Keep the drill's air vents clear of sawdust to avoid overheating the motor.

- Avoid steadying a workpiece by hand; always clamp your stock to a work surface to keep both your hands free to operate the tool.

- Maintain a comfortable, balanced stance when operating the drill; avoid over-reaching.

- Do not force the drill; allow it to bore at its own speed, withdrawing the bit from the hole periodically to clear out the waste.

- Do not wear loose-fitting clothing or jewelry.

DRILLING SAFETY TIPS

- Read your owner's manual carefully before operating any tool.

- Do not use a tool if any of its parts is loose or damaged; inspect blades, bits, and accessories before starting an operation.

- Keep blades and bits clean and sharp; discard any that are chipped or damaged.

- Turn a tool off if it produces an unfamiliar vibration or noise; have the tool serviced before resuming operations.

- Follow the manufacturer's instructions to change blades, bits, or accessories; unplug the tool first.

- Do not force a tool through a cut; this can snap a bit or cause it to veer off course. Allow the blade or bit to cut at its own speed.

- Make sure that any keys and adjusting wrenches are removed from the chuck before turning it on.

- Do not use a tool for extended periods of time without allowing it to cool.

CHAPTER 4:

Sharpening Drill Bits

Drilling with a dull bit takes unnecessary time and effort and can break the bit, cause the drill to slip or ruin a drill motor.

Small, inexpensive bits should be discarded and replaced while dull, larger, more costly bits should be sharpened. And though a professional sharpener can do the job for you, you can easily do the job yourself.

Bits with delicate edges and complex anatomies must be sharpened by hand, preferably with files and whetstones especially fitted to the particular bit, such as triangular stones and files for a countersink bit.

To restore the cutting edges of twist and spade bits, use a grinding wheel with a tool rest and a few simple accessories. A jig sets the correct angles for a twist bit, and a drill gauge checks the angles and lip lengths of the sharpened bit; a stop collar that sets a bit firmly against the tool rest enables you to grind the wings of a spade bit symmetrically.

Always store your bits in partitioned boxes or canvas rolls, and clean them regularly to retard the dulling process. Fine sandpaper and an emery cloth will remove rust and wood sap. To clean the twist of a bit, dip a short length of manila rope in kerosene, then in powdered pumice (available at drugstores), and wrap it around the flutes; to clean the screw point of an auger bit, use a piece of stiff paper.

CUTTING ANGLES

Twist Bit

Two ridges called "lands" spiral around the central shaft, or web, of a twist bit. At the cutting end, the lands are ground to meet at an angle of 118° (82° on some special wood bits), forming two flats, called point surfaces, that converge along a center chisel edge. The front edge of each point surface, called the cutting lip, is slightly higher than the back edge, or heel. The clearance between the two allows the body of the bit to follow easily behind the lips as they cut away wood; the shavings move along the spirals of the lands and out of the hole.

Cutting Lips   Web

Land

The cutting lips are naturally the first parts of the bit to dull—the edges of the lips become slightly rounded, their clearance above the heels decreases and the bit binds and overheats.

Spade Bit

This flat-bladed bit has a point, or spur, that bites into the wood and steadies the bit on center while winglike cutting lips chisel the hole. The edges of the lips and the spur are beveled at an angle of 8°; on most spade bits the lips are perpendicular to the axis of the bit, but in some they are set at an angle. On a dull spade bit the bevels are slightly rounded and the cutting lips slightly unequal and out of line.

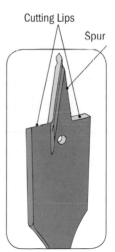

Cutting Lips

Spur

TWIST BIT

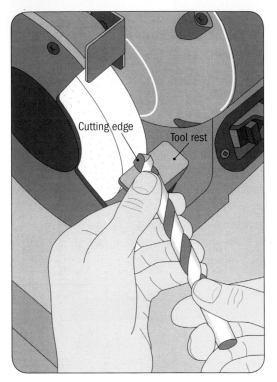

Cutting edge

Tool rest

Holding the bit between the index finger and thumb of one hand, set it on the grinder's tool rest and advance it toward the wheel until your index finger contacts the tool rest. Tilt the shaft of the bit down and to the left so that one of the cutting edges, or lips, is square to the wheel (above). Rotate the bit clockwise to grind the lip evenly. Periodically check the angle of the cutting edge, and try to maintain the angle at about 60°. Repeat for the second cutting edge. Wipe bits occasionally with oil to prevent rust.

TWIST BIT *(continued)*

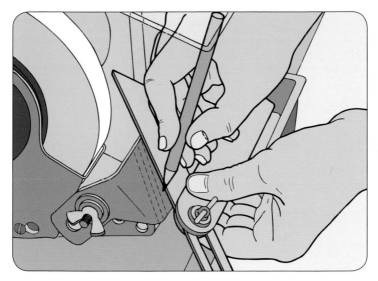

Use a T-bevel and a pencil to draw a line across the tool rest of the grinding wheel at an angle to the face of the wheel that is half of the correct angle for the bit tip—for most twist bits, set the T-bevel to 59°; for special wood bits, to 41°. To the left of this line, at ¼-inch intervals, lay out several parallel lines at an angle 12° less than the first—usually this will be a 47° angle. Use a C clamp to secure a small block of wood to the tool rest, at the right of and flush with the 59° line.

For twist bits smaller than ⅛ inch, omit the parallel lines but adjust the tool rest so that the back edge is 12° lower than the front edge.

TWIST BIT *(continued)*

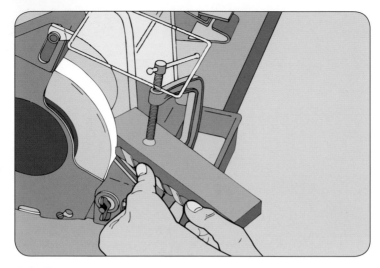

Grinding

Wearing safety goggles or a face mask, start the motor and let the grinding wheel run until it reaches a steady speed. Hold the shank of the twist bit in your right hand and use your left to position the bit against the guide block with one cutting lip perfectly horizontal. Slowly move the bit forward until it makes contact with the wheel, then simultaneously rotate the shank of the bit clockwise and swing the entire bit parallel to the 47° lines. Time the movements so that when the bit reaches the 47° position you have rolled from the cutting lip to the heel of a point surface.

Position the bit with the other cutting lip horizontal and grind the second point surface in the same way. Alternate the passes between the point surfaces, grinding each equally until the bit is sharp. After each two or three passes, stop to cool the bit.

Position a bit smaller than ⅛ inch in the same way, but do not swing or rotate the bit.

TWIST BIT *(continued)*

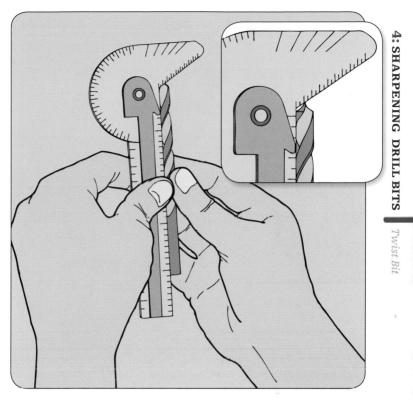

Checking Angles

Set the bit in the lip corner of a drill gauge to compare the lengths of the cutting lips, then turn the bit slightly to check the clearance at the heels (inset). If the lips or clearances are unequal, regrind the bit.

TWIST BIT *(continued)*

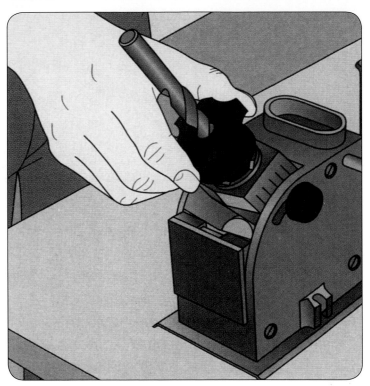

Sharpening Machine

Set up the sharpening machine following the manufacturer's instructions. Adjust the angle block to the appropriate angle for the bit to be sharpened and insert the bit in the depth gauge. The gauge enables you to secure the bit at the correct height in the holder. Fit the bit holder over the bit (above) and use it to remove the bit from the gauge. Now secure the bit and holder to the angle block. Turn on the device and, holding the drill bit steady, slowly rotate the bit holder a full 360° against the stone inside the jig. Apply light pressure; too much force will overheat the bit.

SPADE BIT

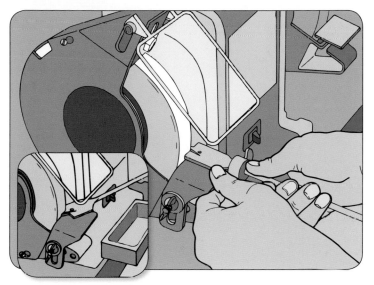

Edge Bevel

Set the tool rest at an angle of 8° to the horizontal, with the higher end facing the grinding wheel, and tighten a stop collar on the shank of a spade bit so that when the stop bears against the edge of the rest, the bit's cutting lips will bear against the wheel face. Hold the bit flat on the tool rest and apply a cutting lip, bevel facing down, to the wheel face. When one lip has been ground, flip the bit to grind the other lip. To grind the bevels at the edges of the spur, swing the bit about 90° and guide it against the wheel freehand (inset). Flip the bit to grind the opposite spur edge, taking care to grind both edges equally so that the spur remains centered.

Remove burrs on the spurs and lips with one or two light strokes of a whetstone on the flat faces.

SPADE BIT *(continued)*

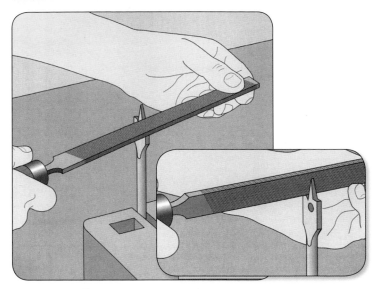

Filing Cutting Edges

Secure the bit in a bench vise and use a smooth single-cut mill file to touch up the two cutting edges. File on the push stroke (above), tilting the handle down slightly to match the angle of the cutting edges; between 5° and 10° is typical. Then touch up the cutting edges on either side of the point the same way (inset), taking care not to alter its taper. Do not remove too much metal at the base of the point, as this will weaken the bit.

BRAD POINT BIT

Filing Chip Lifters

Clamp the bit upright in a bench vise and file the inside faces of the two chip lifters as you would those of a Forstner bit (page 35). For a brad-point bit, however, use a triangular needle file (right), honing until each cutting edge is sharp and each chip lifter is flat.

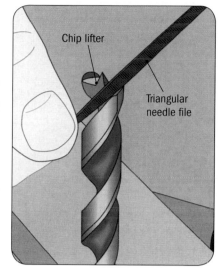

Chip lifter

Triangular needle file

Cutting Spurs

Use the needle file to hone the inside faces of the bit's two cutting spurs. Hold the tool with both hands and file towards the bradpoint until each spur is sharp (right).

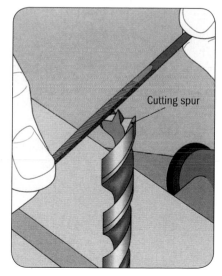

Cutting spur

MULTISPUR BIT

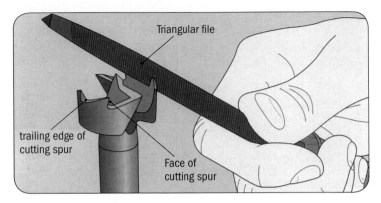

Triangular file

trailing edge of
cutting spur

Face of
cutting spur

Filing Cutting Spurs

Secure the bit upright in a bench vise and use a triangular file to hone
the leading edge, or face, of each spur (above). File with each push
stroke, towards the bit's brad point, tilting the handle of the file down
slightly. Then file the trailing edge, or back, of each spur the same
way. File all the spurs by the same amount so that they remain at the
same height. Make sure you do not over-file the cutting spurs; they are
designed to be 1/32 inch longer than the chip lifters.

Brad Point

File the chip lifters as you would those
of a Forstner bit (page 35). Then, file the
brad-point until it is sharp (right).

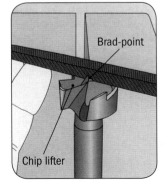

Brad-point

Chip lifter

FORSTNER BITS

Inside Bevel

To touch up a Forstner bit, true the top edge of the bit's rim with a file, removing any nicks. If the beveled edges of the cutting spurs inside the rim are uneven, grind them using an electric drill fitted with a rotary grinding attachment. Secure the bit in a bench vise as shown and grind the edges until they are all uniform (right).

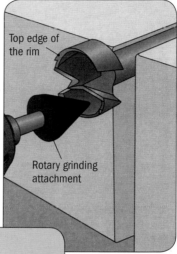

Top edge of the rim

Rotary grinding attachment

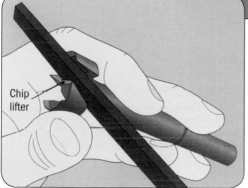

Chip lifter

Chip Lifters

Use a single-cut mill file to lightly file the inside faces of the cutters. Hold the file flat against one of the cutters—also known as chip lifters—and make a few strokes along the surface (above). Repeat with the other cutter. Finish the job by honing the beveled edges inside the rim with a slipstone.

The portable electric drill may not be the first tool that springs to mind when you think of joinery. Nevertheless, for any method of joinery requiring a cavity cut to an exact depth, the drill is a workable choice. It is especially practical for mortise-and-tenon and dowel joints.

For the mortise-and-tenon, the tool will rough out a mortise, although you will need to square the corners with a chisel. A stop collar or a depth guide will guarantee that the bottom of the cavity will be even and level.

A brad-point bit will produce the best results. Choose one with diameter equal to the width of the mortise outline. Its best to cut the tenon first and then use it to mark the dimensions of the mortise.

A drill can perform all the steps needed to prepare stock for a dowel joint. The key to an accurate joint is to center the dowel holes on the workpiece; otherwise, the two pieces being joined will be out of alignment.

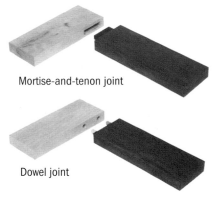

Mortise-and-tenon joint

Dowel joint

DRILLED MORTISE

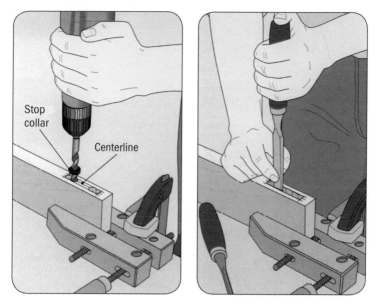

Stop collar

Centerline

Clamp the workpiece in handscrews, then secure the stock to a work surface as shown, with the mortise outline facing up. Mark a line through the center of the outline to help you align the bit. Install a stop collar and adjust the drilling depth to correspond to the length of the tenon. With the bit directly over the centerline, bore a hole at each end of the mortise outline; hold the drill with both hands to keep the tool perpendicular to the edge of the stock. Then make a series of overlapping holes (left) to remove as much waste as possible. Square the mortise with a chisel, keeping the blade perfectly vertical and its beveled edge facing the inside of the mortise (right).

DOWELS

Many woodworkers use dowels to help with the alignment of boards in a panel. One of the problems in using this technique is that the wood pins have to be precisely centered on the edges of the boards to be joined. In the photo at left, location points have been made for the dowels—one about 3 inches from each end of the boards and one in the middle. A line is then scribed across the points with a cutting gauge set to one-half the thickness of the stock. The lines intersect at the center of the board edges, guaranteeing perfect placement of the dowels.

DOWELS *(continued)*

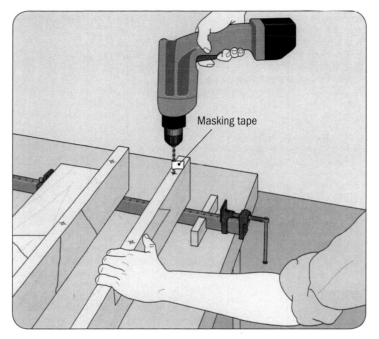

Masking tape

Boring

Locate points for dowels on the board edges. To avoid splitting boards with the pins, use grooved dowels that are no more than one-half as thick as the stock. Fit a drill with a bit the same diameter as the dowels, then wrap a strip of masking tape around the bit to mark the drilling depth, which should be slightly more than one-half the length of the dowels. Keep the drill perpendicular to the board edge as you bore each hole (above), withdrawing the bit when the masking tape touches the stock. (Although the drill press can also be used to bore the holes, keeping longer boards steady on the machine's table may prove difficult.)

DOWELS *(continued)*

Mating Holes

Insert a dowel center the same diameter as the dowels in each of the holes (right), then set the boards flat on the clamps with the triangle mark facing you. Align the ends of the boards and butt

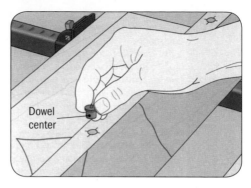

Dowel center

the edge of the second board against that of the first. The pointed ends of the dowel centers will punch impressions on the wood, providing starting points for the mating dowel holes. Bore these holes to the same depth as in step 1, then repeat the procedure for the third board.

Gluing Up

Apply glue to the board the same way as when edge gluing. Then use a pencil tip to dab a small amount of adhesive in each dowel hole. Avoid spreading glue directly on the dowels; they absorb

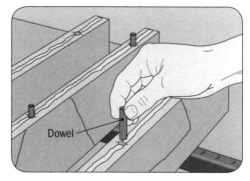

Dowel

moisture quickly and will swell, making them difficult to fit into their holes. Insert dowels, then tap them into final position using a hammer. Avoid pounding on the dowels; this may cause a board to split. Close up the joint, then tighten the clamps. Remove the excess glue.

CHAIRS

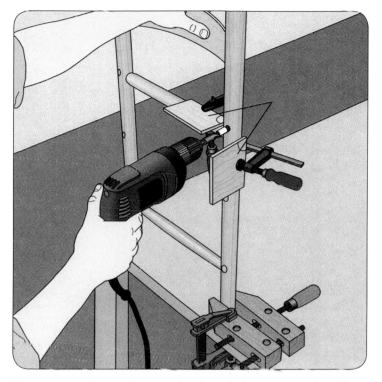

The mortises in the legs for the side rails and stretchers must be drilled at compound angles– they are angled in both the horizontal and vertical planes. Start by securing one of the rear legs in a handscrew and clamping the assembly upright to a work surface. Then use the chair seat and side views, a protractor, and a sliding bevel to determine the drilling angle. But instead of taping two sliding bevels to the stock, cut two square pieces of plywood, clamping one to the leg to indicate the vertical angle and the second to the rail or stretcher for the horizontal angle. Stop drilling when the depth flag contacts the stock.

DOWEL JIG

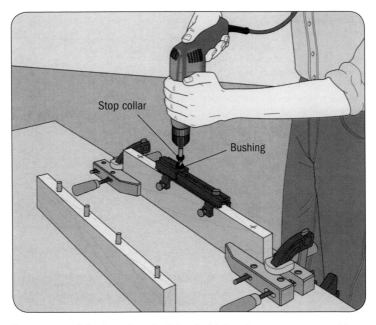

Stop collar

Bushing

Secure one of the boards to be joined with handscrews as you would
when drilling a mortise. Clamp a doweling jig onto the edge of the
workpiece. The model shown centers the dowel holes on the stock and
spaces them at the interval you choose. To avoid splitting the boards,
use grooved dowels that are no more than half the thickness of the
stock. Fit your drill with a bit the same diameter as the dowels, then
install a stop collar to mark the drilling depth, which should be slightly
more than half the length of the dowels. Slide the bushing carrier along
the jig and insert the appropriate bushing in the hole through which you
are planning to drill. The bushing ensures the bit is kept perfectly square
to the board. Holding the drill firmly, bore the hole. Make the remaining
holes for the dowels.

DEPTH GUIDES

Tape Guide

To bore a hole to an exact depth, use a masking tape flag or a depth stop block. If you are using the tape, measure the drilling depth from the tip of the bit, then wrap a strip of tape around its shank. Withdraw the bit when the tape just touches the stock. To use a block, subtract the drilling depth from the length of the

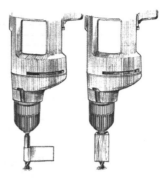

bit protruding from the chuck. Cut a piece of 1-by-1 stock to this length, then bore a hole through its middle. Slip the bit through the block and bore your hole. When the piece of wood touches the workpiece and stops spinning with the bit, retract the tool.

Depth Gauge

To avoid the risk of splitting boards when inserting dowels, use this simple shopmade depth gauge. Rip a 9-inch-long board to a thickness that is exactly one-half the length of the dowels, bore a hole slightly wider than the thickness of the dowels through the gauge near one end. Then place it around each

dowel when you tap it into its hole. The dowel will be at the correct depth when it is flush with the top of the depth gauge.

CENTER-DRILLING JIG

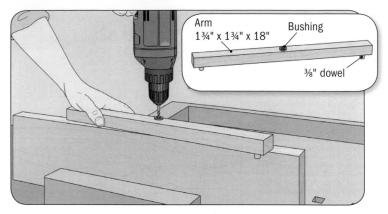

The simple jig shown above enables you to bore holes centered on the edge of a board. The inset provides suggested dimensions. Mark the center of the top face of the arm, and bore a hole for a guide bushing. The hole in the bushing should be the same size as the holes you plan to drill. Turn the arm over and draw a line down its middle. Mark points on the line 1 inch from each end. (Check measurements carefully). Then bore a ⅜-inch-diameter hole halfway through the arm at each mark. Dab some glue into the holes and insert dowels. They should protrude by about ⅜ inch. To use the jig, position it on the workpiece so that the dowels butt against opposite faces of the stock. Holding the jig with one hand, fit the drill bit into the bushing and bore the hole.

This jig can be used to drill in the center of a wide board.

POCKET HOLES

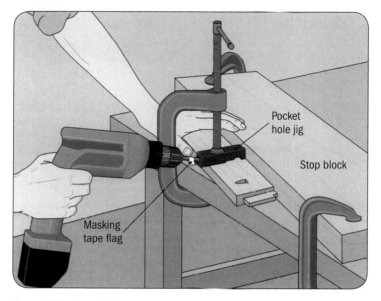

Pocket
hole jig

Stop block

Masking
tape flag

Use a drill to bore holes in two steps with two different brad-point bits:
one slightly larger than the diameter of the screw heads, so they can be
recessed, and one a little larger than the screw shanks to allow a little
movement. Clamp a stop block to a work surface, then fit the first bit on
the drill. Wrap a strip of masking tape around the bit to mark the drilling
depth. Butt the top edge of an upper rail for the cabinet against the stop
block, inside surface up, and clamp a commercial pocket hole jig close
to one end. Holding the rail firmly, bore the hole, stopping when the strip
of tape touches the jig. Reposition the jig to bore another hole at the
middle (above) and a third one near the other end. Fit the second bit on
the drill and bore the clearance holes in the same manner.

CHAPTER 6

Repair and Renovation

Appropriate bits will help your drill make short work of repair projects.

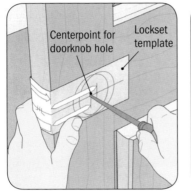

Centerpoint for doorknob hole   Lockset template

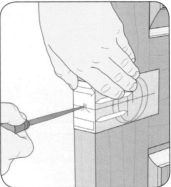

Lockset Layout

Locksets usually come with a template for marking the holes you will need to drill for the latch assembly and doorknobs. Start by marking the height of the knobs on the door—typically 36 inches off the floor. Then tape the template over your mark. Use an awl to mark the doorknob point on the face of the door (above, left)—either 2⅜ or 2¾ inches from the door edge, depending on the model of lockset—then the centerpoint for the latch assembly hole on the door edge (above, right).

DRILLING FOR LOCKSETS

Hole saw

Install a hole saw in your electric drill, referring to the template for the correct diameter. The hole saw shown above features a center pilot bit. Set the point of the pilot bit in the awl mark you made in step 1, then bore into the door until the pilot bit emerges from the other side. Keep the drill perpendicular to the door throughout. Now move to the other side of the door, insert the center pilot bit in the small opening you pierced through the door, and complete the hole. Drilling the hole in two steps will avoid splintering of the wood.

LOCKSET LATCH HOLE

Spade bit

Replace the hole saw with a spade bit; again refer to the template for the appropriate bit diameter. Set the tip of the bit in the awl mark and bore the hole, keeping the drill perpendicular to the door edge (above). For a narrow door, you can clamp wood blocks on the faces of the door on each side of the hole to prevent the wood from splitting. Stop drilling when you reach the handle hole. Some locksets require this hole to be drilled beyond the end of the doorknob hole for clearance.

LATCH ASSEMBLY

Latch Faceplate

Slide the latch plate
assembly into the hole you
drilled in the edge of the
door and set the faceplate
flush against the door
edge. Holding the faceplate
square to the door edge,
trace its outline with
a pencil.

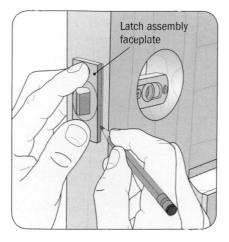

Latch assembly
faceplate

Installing the Latch

Use a chisel to cut a
shallow mortise within
the outline you marked
previously. Mark the screw
holes with an awl. Drill a
pilot hole at each mark.
Slide the latch assembly
in the hole and screw the
faceplate to the door edge.

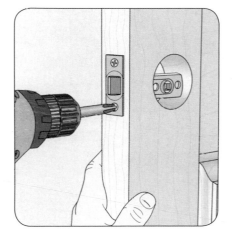

HANDRAIL

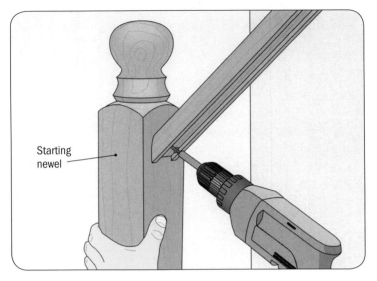

Starting newel

Attaching to Newel

To fasten a handrail to newel posts with screws, hold the rail in position and drill a clearance hole though the rail and a pilot hole into the posts. At the top of the stairs, drill counterbored holes and drive the screws through the top face of the rail. Conceal the screw heads with wood plugs. At the bottom, work from the underside of the rail and countersink the screws (above)

HANDRAIL *(continued)*

Attaching to Wall

Cut the handrail to length as the handrail. The model shown at right features a return that serves as a tactile reminder to the visually impaired that they are arriving at the top or bottom of the stairs. Locate the studs along the wall side of the stair. Then position the floating handrail against the wall parallel to the other handrail and mark the stud locations on it. Screw commercial wall brackets to the underside of the rail (top) at the stud location marks at intervals specified by your local building code. Reposition the handrail on the wall, mark the screw holes, bore pilot holes into the wall, and fasten the rail in place (bottom).

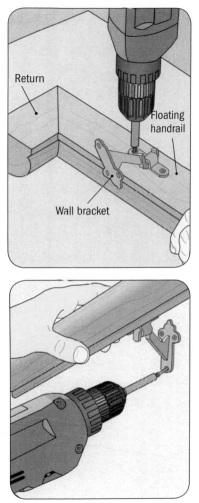

Return

Floating handrail

Wall bracket

CHAPTER 7

Drill Press

Originally designed for the metalworking trades, the drill press has found a second home in woodworking shops, where it has been a thoroughly welcome addition.

Imagine trying to bore precise holes without it and you have an idea of how essential the tool is in exacting pursuits such as cabinetmaking. The drill press also does duty as a sander and mortiser and yet—despite its versatility—it takes up only a few square feet of workshop space and is relatively inexpensive. Many experts consider this machine a wise acquisition for the woodworker with limited space and budget.

One feature that distinguishes the drill press from other woodworking machines is its speed variability. The range for a typical ½-horsepower motor extends from 400 to 4500 spindle

Although the drill press is used primarily to bore holes, it can also perform other woodworking tasks, such as sanding curved surfaces.

DRILL PRESS *(continued)*

revolutions per minute (rpm). Having the ability to vary the speed allows you to bore with equal efficiency through softwood and hardwood, ranging in thickness from a fraction of an inch to 3 or 4 inches thick.

As a rule of thumb, the thicker the stock or the larger the drill bit diameter, the slower the speed.

Some machines feature a knob that provides infinitely variable speed adjustments. On other machines, speeds are adjusted by shifting a belt to different steps on two pulleys.

Drill presses are rated according to the distance from the center of the chuck to the column, a factor that determines the widest workpiece a machine is capable of handling. A 15-inch drill press, for example, can cut a hole through the center of a workpiece that is 15 inches in diameter. The distance from the chuck to the column is one half that diameter, or 7½ inches.

Most drill presses for the home workshop are in the 11- to 16-inch range and are powered by ½- to ¾-horsepower motors.

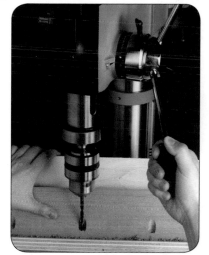

Equipped with the appropriate jigs and accessories, the drill press can bore a variety of holes with a precision unmatched by hand tools. Here, a shopmade jig allows a woodworker to drill a series of angled holes in a rail. The holes will house and conceal the screws that connect the rail to a tabletop.

CHOOSING A DRILL PRESS

Drill presses come in various models and sizes, but the basic design is the same: A steel column 3 or so inches in diameter serves as a backbone to support a table and a motor that drives a spindle. The standard spindle is attached to a geared chuck with a ½-inch capacity whose jaws grip the shank of a drill bit or one of a variety of other accessories up to ½-inch in diameter. Other spindles allow the drill press to accept router bits, molding cutters, and mortising attachments. The column is held upright by a heavy base, usually made of cast iron, but can be bolted to the shop floor.

The two most common types of drill presses are the floor model and the bench variety, as distinguished by length of the column. Because the table of a drill press can be positioned anywhere along the length of the column, floor models can handle longer workpieces. However, you can—to some extent—overcome the limitations of a bench-model drill press by swinging around the head of the machine. With the spindle extended beyond the edge of the workbench, the effective column length is the distance from the chuck to the shop floor.

While most drill presses have tables that tilt, the radial arm drill press features a head that rotates more than 90° right and left. Such tools can perform jobs impossible on conventional drill presses, including drilling through the center of a 32-inch-diameter circle.

DRILL PRESS ANATOMY

Belt guard Protects operator's fingers from turning belts

Belt tension lever Slides motor along track to slacken or tension belts

Belt tension lock knob Locks motor in position once belt tension is set

On/off switch Removable toggle prevents accidental start-up

▲DELTA

Quill Movable sleeve attached to spindle and chuck; quill travel determines maximum drilling depth—typically, 4 inches

Spindle Hold drill bits and accessories for drilling; tightened with a geared key

Chuck Holds drill bits and accessories fro drilling; tightened with a geared key

Depth-stop lock handle For setting drilling depths; when locked, prevents quill from descending past a set point

Feed lever Lowers quill; adjustable coil spring automatically returns lever to original position

Table lock Holds table in fixed position on column

Table height adjustment handle

Table Raised and lowered to accommodate workpiece and drilling depth; most tables can be tilted up to 45° left and right for boring angled holes

Table rotation lock handle Allows table to be turned on its axis to position work-piece under spindle

Column Supports table and head of drill press

Drill Press Anatomy

SAFETY

Like any stationary power tool, the drill press has to be kept in adjustment to perform well. Before switching a machine on, check it carefully. Make sure all nuts and lock knobs are tightened. Even if you bought your machine new, there is no guarantee that it is perfectly ready to run. Check regularly that the table is square to the spindle.

There are also adjustments that have to be made depending on the particular job at hand, beginning with setting the drilling speed. The speed is changed either by turning a knob or by shifting the position of the belt—or belts—that connect the motor pulley to the spindle pulley.

The drill press has a reputation as a "safe" machine. Nevertheless, it is possible to have accidents on the drill press. Unlike the table saw, a drill press will not kick back, but it can send a small workpiece spinning out of control if the stock is not clamped properly. Always wear eye protection.

Choosing—or Making —the Right Clamp

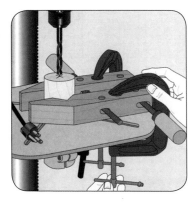

To prevent the drill bit from grabbing the workpiece and spinning it uncontrollably, always clamp small or irregularly shaped stock securely to the table before boring into it. When a conventional clamping setup does not work—as for the cylinder shown—improvise. Cut opposing V-shaped wedges out of a handscrew and clamp the cylinder in the handscrew, then use C clamps to secure the handscrew to the table.

SETTING UP

Drill presses have a reputation as workhorse machines that rarely—if ever—require maintenance. And yet they can slip out of alignment just as easily as any other stationary power tool.

Most drill press problems are found in the chuck and table. A table that is not square to the spindle is the most common problem, and is easily remedied. Runout, or wobble, is a more serious problem, and can be traced to the spindle or chuck. If the problem lies with the spindle, it can often be fixed simply by striking the spindle with a hammer until it is true; if the chuck is at fault, it must be removed and replaced.

Do not neglect the drill press belts and pulleys in your maintenance. Check the belts for wear, and always keep them tensioned properly. Periodically check the bearings in the pulleys, and replace them if they become worn.

Spindle pulley Turns spindle; features different steps to provide a range of speeds.

Belt Transfers power from motor pulley to jackshaft pulley; (other belt transfers power from jackshaft to spindle pulley).

Jackshaft pulley Intermediate pulley connected to spindle pulley so as to increase the range of speeds; driven by motor pulley.

Motor pulley Driven by motor; connected by belt to drive jackshaft pulley. Features different steps to provide a range of speeds.

DRILLING SPEED

Loosen the belt tension lock knob and turn the belt tension lever counterclockwise to shift the motor toward the spindle pulley and slacken the belts. To set the rpm, position each belt on the correct steps of the pulleys, taking care not to pinch your fingers. (Refer to the drilling speed chart on the inside of the belt guard.) To set the belt tension, turn the tension lever clockwise while pressing the belt connected to the motor pulley until it flexes about 1 inch out of line. Tighten the belt tension lock knob.

The speed of many drill presses is changed by a system of belts and pulleys housed in the top of the tool. These drill presses feature a lever that loosens the belts for changing and tightens them to set the correct tension.

SQUARING THE TABLE

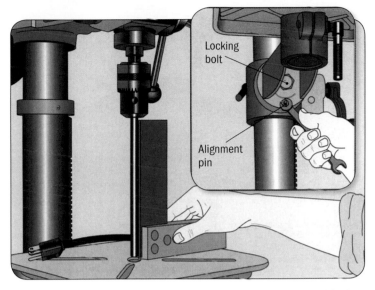

Locking bolt

Alignment pin

Install an 8-inch-long steel rod in the chuck as you would a drill bit, then raise the table until it almost touches the rod. Butt a try square against the rod as shown; the blade should rest flush against the rod (above). If there is a gap, remove the alignment pin under the table using a wrench (inset). Loosen the table locking bolt. Swivel the table to bring the rod flush against the square, then tighten the locking bolt. (Because the holes for the alignment pin will now be offset, do not reinstall the pin. The locking bolt is sufficient to hold the table securely in place.)

CHECKING ALIGNMENT

To check whether the table is square to the spindle, make a 90° bend at each end of a 12-inch length of wire coat hanger. Insert one end of the wire in the chuck and adjust the table height until the other end of the wire just touches the table. Rotate the wire; it should barely scrape the table at all points during the rotation. If not, remove the alignment pin under the table, loosen the table locking bolt and swivel the table to square it. Tighten the locking bolt.

Checking Alignment

A magnetic-base dial indicator checks the spindle of a drill press for runout—the amount of wobble that the spindle transmits to a bit or accessory. For accurate drilling, the runout should not exceed 0.005 inch. If it does, replace or repair the spindle.

REMOUNTING THE CHUCK

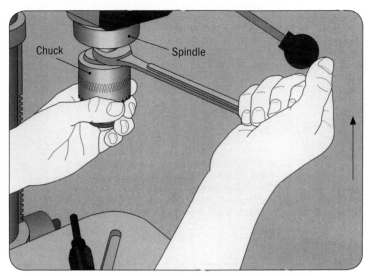

Chuck   Spindle

Chucks are commonly attached to the quill of a drill press with a tapered spindle. (Older models often have chucks that are simply screwed in place.) To remove a faulty chuck that features a tapered spindle, first lower the quill and lock it in place. Fit an open-end wrench around the spindle on top of the chuck and give the wrench a sharp upward blow (above). The chuck should slide out. If not, rotate the spindle and try again. To remount the chuck, press-fit it into the spindle by hand. Then, with the chuck's jaws fully retracted, give the chuck a sharp blow with a wooden mallet.

CHANGING A DRILL BIT

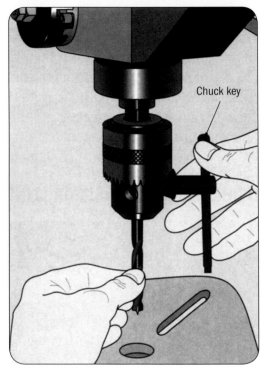

Chuck key

To remove a bit, use the chuck key to loosen the chuck jaws while holding the bit with your other hand. Slip the bit out of the chuck. To install a bit, open the jaws as wide as necessary, then insert the shank in the chuck. Steadying the bit to center it in the jaws, tighten the chuck by hand. Finish tightening using the chuck key (above), fitting it in turn into each hole in the chuck. Remove the chuck key.

ACCESSORIES RACK

To save time searching for chuck keys and drill bits, use a shopmade storage rack. Cut two identical keyhole-shaped pieces of ¾-inch plywood to the dimensions shown here. Use a saber saw or coping saw to cut a circle out of each piece the same diameter as your drill press column. Then saw one piece in half lengthwise to serve as the jig support. The other piece will be the jig top; saw it across the circular cutout. Bore six screw holes for joining the top to its supports. Then, bore holes into the working surface of the jig to hold your bits and accessories shank-end down (right).

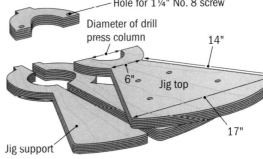

Hole for 1¼" No. 8 screw

Diameter of drill press column

14"

6"

Jig top

17"

Jig support

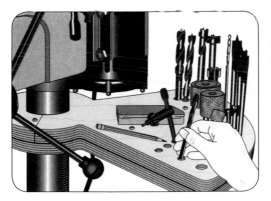

Make sure the jig is turned so it does not obstruct the rotation of the drill press's quill lever.

CHAPTER 8:
Drill Press Operations

Equipped with its tiltable table, the drill press can bore holes at virtually any angle. The steeper the angle, however, the more difficult it is for a brad-point or twist bit to dig into the stock without skating. Choose a Forstner or multispur bit when drilling holes at a very steep angle; both of these cutting accessories feature guiding rims that provide cleaner penetration.

Before drilling, be certain the drill bit lines up over the hole in the table. Otherwise, you risk damaging not only the bit but also the table itself. Most woodworkers also clamp a piece of wood to the drill press table.

For good results you will need to find the right combination of drilling speed and feed pressure—the rate at which you lower the bit into the stock. Too much speed or feed pressure can cause burn marks on the workpiece and bit; too little will dull the bit's cutting edge. With the proper combination, you should be able to cut steadily without having to put undue pressure on the quill feed lever.

HOLE DEPTH

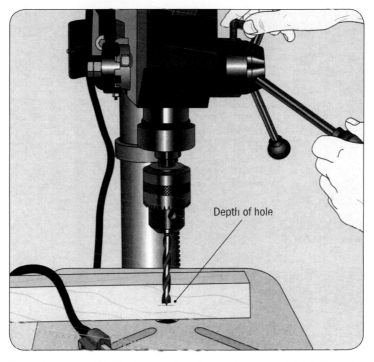

Depth of hole

For a stopped or blind hole—one that does not pass completely through a workpiece—mark a line at the desired depth of the hole on the edge of the stock. Then, lower the quill until the tip of the drill bit reaches the marked line. Hold the quill steady with one hand and, for the model shown, unscrew the depth-stop lock handle with the other hand and turn it counterclockwise as far as it will go (above). Tighten the handle. This will keep the drill press from drilling any deeper than the depth mark.

SPACING JIG

To bore a row of uniformly spaced holes, make a shopmade jig to systematize the task, following the dimensions provided here. Screw the fence to the jig base, flush with one edge, then attach a wood block at the center of the fence to serve as a dowel holder.

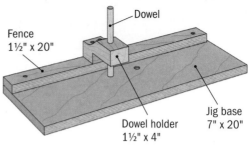

Dowel

Fence
1½" x 20"

Jig base
7" x 20"

Dowel holder
1½" x 4"

To use the jig, set it on the table of your drill press, then mark starting points on the workpiece for the first two holes in the series. Seat the workpiece against the fence of the jig and position the jig to align the bit—preferably a Forstner—over the first drilling mark. Butt a guide block against the back of the jig and clamp it to the table. If you are boring stopped holes, set the drilling depth (below). Bore the first hole, then slide the jig along the guide block and bore a hole through the dowel holder. Fit a dowel through the hole in the holder and into the hole in the workpiece. Slide the jig along the guide block until the second mark on the workpiece is aligned under the bit. Clamp the jig to the table and bore the hole.

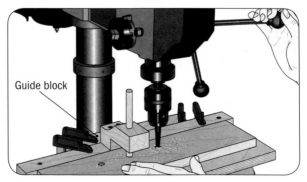

Guide block

DEEP HOLES

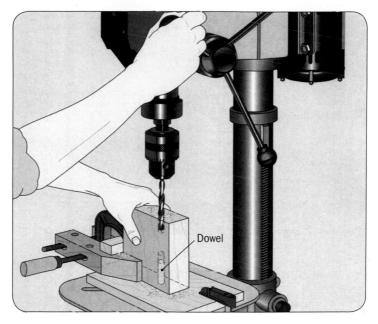

Dowel

The maximum length the quill can be extended—known as the quill stroke—limits most drill presses to boring no more than 4 inches deep at a time. To drill a deeper hole, use an extension bit or, if the hole is less than twice the quill stroke, perform the operation in two stages, as shown above. First, clamp a scrap board to the drill press table and bore a guide hole into it. Then, clamp the workpiece to the board and bore into it as deeply as the quill stroke will allow. Remove the workpiece and fit a dowel into the guide hole in the scrap board. Fit the hole in the workpiece over the dowel and bore into the workpiece from the other side. The dowel ensures the two holes in the workpiece are perfectly aligned.

ANGLED HOLES

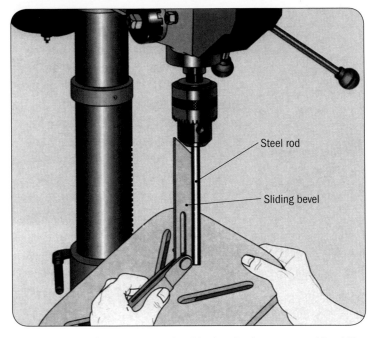

Steel rod

Sliding bevel

Install a straight 8-inch-long steel rod in the chuck as you would a drill bit, then use a protractor to set the drilling angle you need on a sliding bevel. Loosen the table as you would to square it (page 59). Then butt the bevel against the steel rod and swivel the table until the table rests flush against the handle of the bevel (above). Remove the rod from the chuck and tighten the locking bolt. After installing the drill bit, set the drilling depth (page 65) to prevent the bit from reaching the table. For added protection, clamp a piece of wood to the table.

TILTING TABLE JIG

To bore angled holes without tilting the table, use a tilting jig, shopbuilt from ¾-inch plywood. Refer to the illustration at right for dimensions. Connect the jig top to the base using two sturdy butt hinges. Cut a ½-inch-wide slot in the support brackets, then screw each one to the top; secure the brackets to the base with wing nuts and hanger bolts.

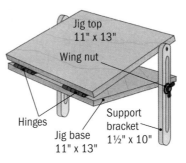

To use the jig, center it under the spindle. Clamp the base to the table. Loosen the wing nuts and set the angle of the jig as you would the table, but without removing the alignment pin or loosening the table locking bolt. Tighten the wing nuts, clamp the workpiece to the jig, and bore the hole (below).

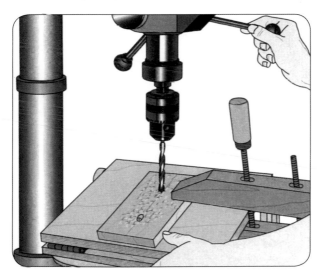

V-BLOCK

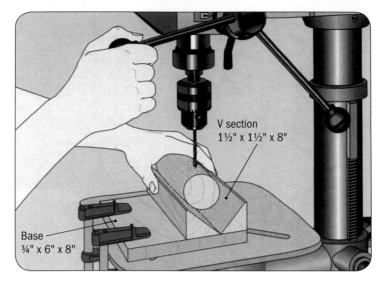

V section
1½" x 1½" x 8"

Base
¾" x 6" x 8"

The safest way to bore into a cylinder is to secure it in a shopmade
V-block jig. Make the V section of the jig by bevel cutting a 2-by-2
lengthwise using a table saw or band saw. Then, screw the two cut
pieces to the base to form a V. Position the jig on the table so
the drill bit touches the center of the V when the quill is extended.
Clamp the base to the table, seat the workpiece in the jig and bore
the hole (above).

DOWEL CUTTER

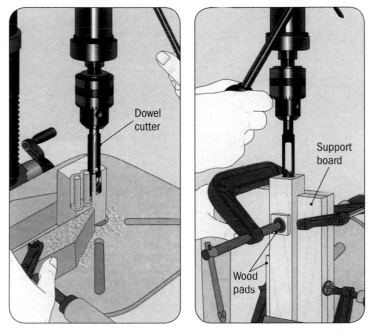

Dowel cutter

Support board

Wood pads

Dowel Cutter

To cut dowels, clamp a block of wood to the table and bore into its end grain to the required depth with a dowel cutter (left). Free the dowels by cutting through the block with a table saw or a band saw. If you will be using the dowels for joinery, crimp their ends with the serrated jaws of pliers; this will provide the glue with an escape route and ensure proper glue coverage.

To cut an integral tenon on a long workpiece, tilt the table 90° and clamp the workpiece to the table, using pads to protect the wood. Also clamp a support board to the workpiece and to the table. Use a dowel cutter to bore to the required depth (right), then saw away the waste to expose the tenon.

POCKET HOLE JIG

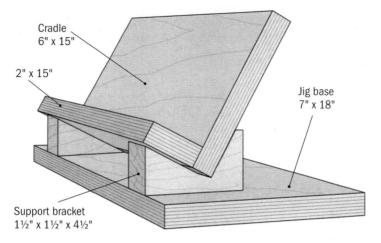

Cradle
6" x 15"

2" x 15"

Jig base
7" x 18"

Support bracket
1½" x 1½" x 4½"

Pocket holes are commonly used with screws to attach rails to a tabletop. They are drilled at an angle and solve the problem of having to screw straight through a 3- or 4-inch-wide rail. A pocket hole jig, shopbuilt from ¾-inch plywood, makes simple work of such openings. For the jig, screw the two sides of the cradle together to form an L. Then cut a 90° wedge from each support bracket so that the wide side of the cradle will sit at an angle about 15° from the vertical. Screw the brackets to the jig base and glue the cradle to the brackets.

To use the jig, seat the workpiece in the cradle with the side that will be drilled facing out. Bore the holes in two steps with two different bits: Use a Forstner bit twice the width of the screw heads for the entrance holes and a brad-point bit slightly wider than the width of the screw shanks for the exit holes. (The wider brad-point bit allows for wood expansion and contraction.)

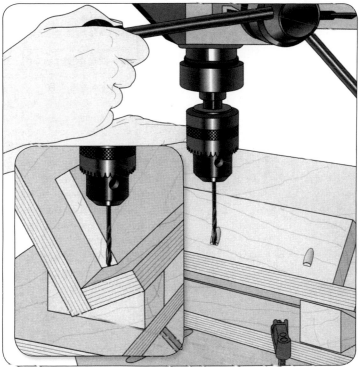

To begin the process, install the brad-point bit and, with the machine off, lower the bit with the feed lever, then butt the end of the workpiece against the bit. Position the jig to align the bit with the center of the bottom edge of the workpiece (inset). Clamp the jig to the table and replace the brad-point bit with the Forstner bit.

Holding the workpiece firmly in the jig, feed the bit slowly to bore the holes just deep enough to recess the screw heads. Then, install the brad-point bit and bore through the workpiece to complete the pocket holes.

MORTISING

The mortise-and-tenon joint is commonly used to join rails to legs on desks, tables, and chairs. Like most joints, the mortise-and-tenon can be cut by hand. But for ease and efficiency in carving out mortises, the drill press equipped with a mortising attachment has become the tool of choice. The attachment consists of a bit that rotates inside a square-edged chisel. The bit cuts a round hole; the chisel then punches the corners square. The matching tenon can be cut easily on a table saw.

Chisels come in different sizes to cut mortises in a variety of widths. The depth is set with the drill press depth-stop; ⅞ inch is typical. It is important to make sure the attachment is adjusted to keep the workpiece square to the chisel.

The drilling speed for mortising depends on both the type of stock and the size of the chisel. The larger the chisel, the slower the speed, especially when you are drilling into hardwood.

A typical mortising attachment consists of a chisel holder (1) that is secured to the drill press quill by machine bolts at the top of the holder. Screws, washers, and wingnuts hold the fence (2) and the hold-down bracket (3) in place on the table. The vertical bar (4) supports the hold-down arm (5), which, along with the hold-down rods (6), helps hold the workpiece firmly against the fence.

MORTISING *(continued)*

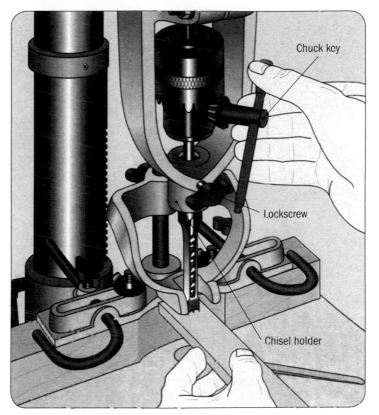

Chuck key

Lockscrew

Chisel holder

Setting the Gap

Insert the chisel into its holder and tighten the lockscrew. Push the bit up through the chisel into the chuck. Hold the tip of the bit level with the bottom of the chisel with a scrap of wood, then lower the bit by $\frac{1}{32}$ inch. This ensures proper clearance between the tip of the bit and the points of the chisel. Tighten the chuck jaws.

MORTISING *(continued)*

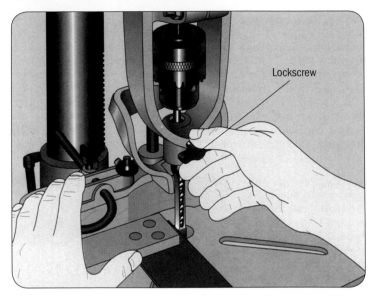

Lockscrew

Adjusting the Chisel

The chisel must be square to the mortising attachment fence or
the mortises you cut will angle off-center, producing ill-fitting joints.
To make sure that the chisel is properly aligned, butt a try square
against the fence and chisel. The square should rest flush against
both. If it does not, loosen the chisel holder lockscrew just enough
to allow you to rotate the chisel and bring it flush against the square.
Do not raise or lower the chisel while making the adjustment. Tighten
the lockscrew.

MORTISING *(continued)*

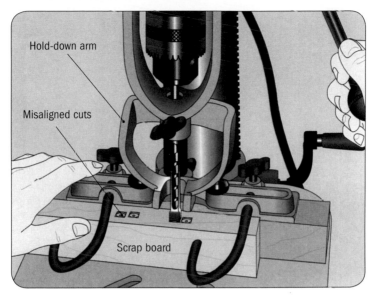

Hold-down arm

Misaligned cuts

Scrap board

Cutting the Mortise

Outline the mortise on the workpiece, centering the marks between the edges of the stock. To check whether the mortise chisel will be centered on the workpiece, butt a scrap board the same width and thickness as the workpiece against the mortising attachment fence and secure it with the hold-down rods. Bore a shallow cut into the board. Then, flip the board around and make a second cut next to the first. The cuts should be aligned. If not, shift the fence by one-half the amount that the cuts were misaligned and make two more cuts to repeat the test.

MORTISING *(continued)*

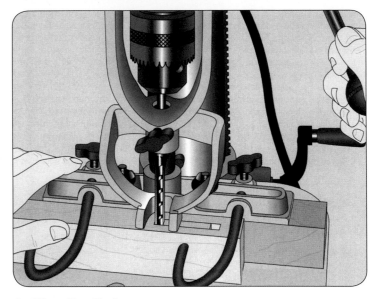

Cutting the Ends

Adjust the hold-down arm and rods to secure the workpiece while allowing it to slide freely along the fence. If you are boring a stopped mortise—one that does not pass completely through the workpiece—set the drilling depth. Make a cut at each end of the planned mortise, feeding the chisel and bit with enough pressure to allow them to dig into the wood without laboring. Retract the chisel often to clear away waste chips and prevent overheating.

MORTISING *(continued)*

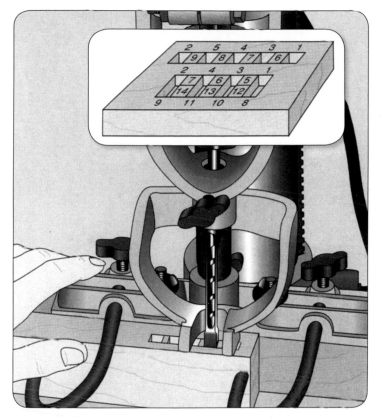

Sequence of Cuts

Make a series of staggered cuts to complete the mortise. Follow the sequence shown in the inset, making a single row of cuts if you are using a chisel equal in width to the mortise, or two parallel rows if the mortise is too wide to be cut in a single pass. In the latter case, use a chisel slightly wider than one-half the width of the mortise.

SANDING

Drill presses make excellent sanders. The machine's table provides good support for the workpiece, holding it at 90° to the sanding drum to produce sanded edges that are square to adjacent surfaces. And with help from some simple jigs, the drill press can sand not only straight surfaces but curved ones as well.

Sanding drums come in diameters ranging from ½ to 3 inches. The shaft of a drum is inserted into the jaws of the chuck and secured in the same way drill bits are installed. Sanding sleeves to cover the drum are available in a variety of grits—from a coarse 40 grit to a fine 220 grit. In most cases, sleeves are changed by loosening a nut at either the top or the bottom of the drum, which reduces the pressure and releases the sandpaper. Remove the old sleeve and slip on the new. Tightening the nut causes the drum to expand and grip the sleeve securely.

As with standard drilling operations, sanding requires a variety of speeds depending on the job. The higher the rpm, the smoother the finish, but high speeds also wears out your sleeves more quickly. Most sanding is done between 1200 and 1500 rpm. Sanding produces fine dust, so remember to wear a dust mask.

SANDING *(continued)*

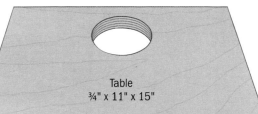

Table
¾" x 11" x 15"

Sanding Table

Sanding drums larger than
⅞ inch in diameter are too
large to fit through the hole
in most drill press tables.
To make full use of the
sanding surface of larger
drums, build a table like
the one shown above. Use
a coping saw, a saber saw,
or an electric drill fitted with
a hole saw to cut a hole in
the plywood top, centering

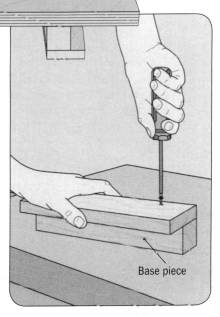

Base piece

the opening 3 inches from the back of the table. Screw the L-shaped
base pieces together from 1-by-3 and 2-by-2 stock, then glue them to
the table.

SANDING *(continued)*

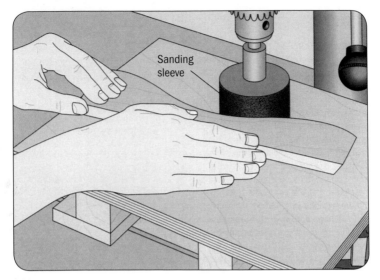

Sanding sleeve

Curved Stock

Clamp the jig base to the drill press table with the hole directly underneath the drum. Adjust the table height to bring the bottom of the sanding sleeve level with the jig. Holding the workpiece firmly, feed it at a uniform speed in a direction opposite the rotation of the sanding drum. To avoid burning or gouging the workpiece, feed it with a smooth, continuous motion. As segments of the sanding sleeve wear out, raise the drill press table to bring a fresh surface to bear.

SANDING *(continued)*

Pattern Sanding

Used in conjunction with the auxiliary sanding table, a shopmade pattern sanding jig will allow you to sand parallel curves. To make the jig, cut a U-shaped wedge out of the

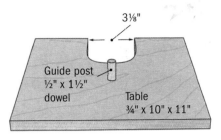

3⅛"

Guide post
½" x 1½"
dowel

Table
¾" x 10" x 11"

plywood table the same size as the hole in the sanding table jig. Then, use a ½-inch Forstner bit to bore a hole the same distance from the bottom of the U as the width of the stock that will be sanded. Insert a dowel into the hole to serve as a guide post.

To use the jig, clamp it to the auxiliary sanding table so that opposite edges of the workpiece rest against the dowel and the sanding drum. Remove the workpiece, then switch on the drill press. Feed the workpiece slowly but continuously against the direction of sanding drum rotation with your left hand while guiding it with your right hand.

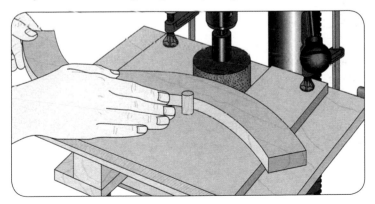

Sanding

Kitchen cabinets can have a professional look without hiring a professional to install them. A portable drill is critical for cabinet assembly and installation.

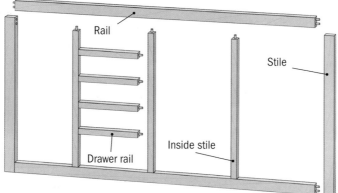

Rail

Stile

Inside stile

Drawer rail

Face Frame

A face frame is a solid wood grid applied to kitchen cabinets. They are not essential; in fact they are absent on European-style cabinets, whose concealed, micro-adjustable hinges help install doors that seamlessly cover the entire cabinet front. However, face frames can add a traditional look to a kitchen and they do make a plywood cabinet much stronger.

Add an extra ½ inch to stiles positioned next to walls; doing so allows you to scribe and trim the stile if the wall is out-of-plumb.

DOWEL JOINTS

Use a doweling jig to drill holes for dowels in the face frame members. The model shown at top right aligns the holes in both rails and stiles and holds the bit exactly perpendicular to the wood surface. Set up the jig for the thickness of the face frame stock, then adjust the jig to drill two holes about ½ inch in from either end of one of the stiles. Insert the bushing that matches the dowel diameter into the bushing carrier of the jig, and attach a collet to the drill bit and adjust it to bore a hole ⅟₁₆ inch deeper than half the length of the dowels. (Allow for the thickness of the jig and bushing when making this measurement.) Clamp a stile in your workbench and place the jig on the stile, aligning it with one end of the workpiece. Set the bushing carrier in the appropriate hole in the doweling jig. Holding the jig steady, drill the hole. Repeat to drill the second hole, then bore the holes at the opposite end of the stile, in both ends of all rails (below right), and in any inside stiles that also require dowel holes.

Insert dowels in the drawer rails and inside stiles first, then in the outer stiles. To insert the dowels, clamp the appropriate frame member to your bench, spread glue on one end of the dowel, then tap it home with a mallet. Assemble the frame.

WOOD PLUGS

If you are installing your face frames with screws, counterbore the fasteners and cover their heads with wood plugs. Position the frame in place as you would for face-nailing, drill and counterbore screw holes, then drive the screws in place. To make the plugs, install a plug cutter the same diameter as the counterbored holes in your drill press. Choosing some wood that matches the frame stock for grain and color, bore as many plugs as you need in the stock (top right).

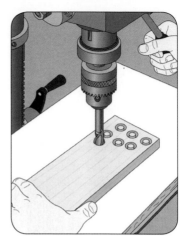

Pry the plugs free with a screwdriver or narrow chisel. To install the plugs, apply glue in the hole, then tap the plug in place. Trim the excess with a chisel. Holding the chisel bevel-side up on the frame, remove the waste in fine shavings (bottom right) until the plug is perfectly flush. This will produce a much cleaner surface than if the plug were sanded flush.

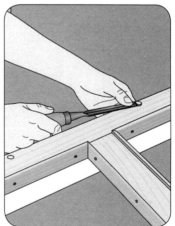

WOOD PLUGS *(continued)*

Preparing the Surface

An effective way to repair deep surface defects like screw holes or burns is to fill the damage with a wood plug. Start by drilling a hole into the surface to accept the plug. Fit an electric drill with a brad-point or Forstner bit slightly larger than the defect, center the bit over the damage, and bore a ½-inch-deep hole. Keep the drill vertical throughout and avoid boring completely through the workpiece.

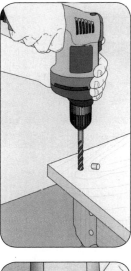

Installing the Plug

To ensure the plug blends with the color and grain of the surface, make your own from a matching piece of wood. Using a plug cutter on your drill press, cut several plugs from the face of the board, making sure their diameter is identical to that of the hole you drilled in step 1. The plugs should be slightly longer than the depth of the hole. Compare each plug with the surface and choose the one that blends in best. Spread glue on the plug and in the

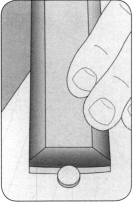

hole, insert the plug, and tap it in place with a mallet. Trim the plug flush with the surface using a chisel, then sand the surface smooth.

COUNTERTOP

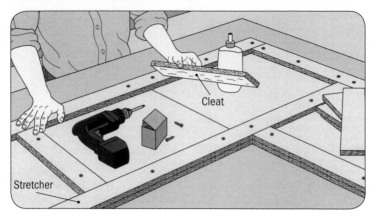

Cleat

Stretcher

Counter substrates are usually made of ¾-inch medium-density fiberboard, chosen for its dimensional stability. To double the perceived thickness of the countertop and increase its strength, build up the substrate with stretchers and cleats. First cut the substrate to size, making sure to include the amount of overhang; typically ¾ inch. Then prepare a number of 4-inch-wide stretchers and cleats of the same material as the substrate. Screw the stretchers along the edges of the substrate, then attach cleats between the stretchers, spacing them every 18 to 20 inches. If you are joining two sheets of substrate into an L-shaped countertop, make sure to secure a cleat on the joint.

DRAWER SLIDE

Commercial slides have simplified the installation of drawers to the point where that they have virtually supplanted all other drawer-hanging hardware, and for good reason. The slides are simple to install and can be secured with only three or four screws. Some commercial slides even allow for fine tuning and can be adjusted vertically after the screws have been installed.

For the kitchen user, commercial drawer slides also offer unmatched durability. Good quality side-mounted slides are rigorously tested; they must open and close flawlessly at least 100,000 times and support a load of 150 pounds when fully extended. Bottom-mounted slides cannot bear nearly as much weight, but are considerably less expensive.

Some bottom-mounted drawer slides can extend a drawer its full length to display the contents inside.

DRAWER SLIDE *(continued)*

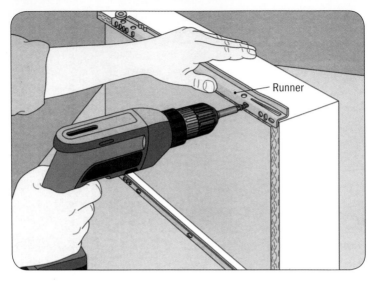

Runner

Bottom Mount

Bottom-mounted slides consist of two parts: a runner that attaches to the bottom of the drawer slide and a track that is secured to the cabinet sides. Before installing the first drawer, place it in front of the case and lay out the slide parts beside it. Make sure you understand where each piece goes and its orientation. To position the runner, set the drawer on its side and butt the runner against the bottom of the drawer side as shown. Inset the hardware $\frac{1}{16}$ inch back from the drawer front so it will not interfere with the false front. Secure the runner from below or from the side. If you are using solid wood or plywood, attach it from the side. If you have chosen Melamine, attach the runner from below. In both cases, drill pilot holes first to avoid splitting the material.

DRAWER SLIDE *(continued)*

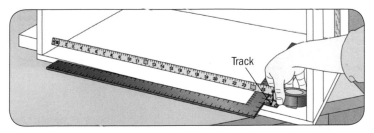

Track

Position Tracks

Once you have determined the spacing of the drawers, position the tracks for bottom-mounted slides on the sides of the cabinet. Place a track on the cabinet side, using a framing square to hold it at a right angle to the cabinet front. For face frame cabinets, place the track almost flush with the front edge of the cabinet; for frameless cabinets, inset the drawer by the thickness of the false front stock; typically about ¾ inch. Measure out the appropriate drawer height then move the square and track together to align the bottom of the track with this distance. Mark the predrilled holes in the track onto the cabinet side.

Fasten Tracks

Drill a pilot hole at each of the marks you made in step 1, wrapping a piece of tape around the drill bit to ensure the screws do not pass through the cabinet's side. Fasten the track in place with a screw in each hole. If you have multiple drawers to install at a certain height, cut a plywood spacer to fit between the track and the cabinet bottom. Place all the tracks at the same height without measuring.

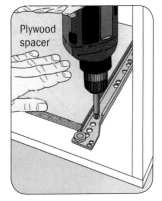

Plywood spacer

DRAWER SLIDE *(continued)*

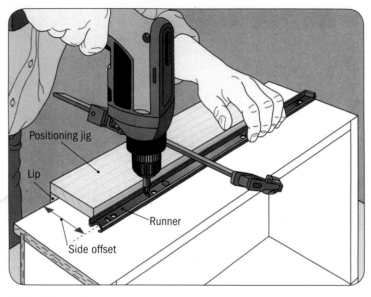

Positioning jig

Lip

Runner

Side offset

Side Mount

Unlike bottom-mounted slides, the runners of a side-mounted drawer slide can be attached to the side of a drawer at any height. To make installation easier, always offset the runner the same distance from the bottom edge of the drawer side. The runner in the illustration was placed 3⅛ inches from the edge, measuring to the center of the runner. Make a simple jig to position all the runners at exactly the same spot on each drawer. Fasten some one-inch-square stock as a lip to a 12-inch length of plywood, then trim the jig to width to hold the runner at the right position as shown. To attach each runner, first separate the runner from the track. Then clamp the jig to the drawer side and hold the runner against it, making sure it is flush with the drawer front. Secure the runner with screws.

DRAWER SLIDE *(continued)*

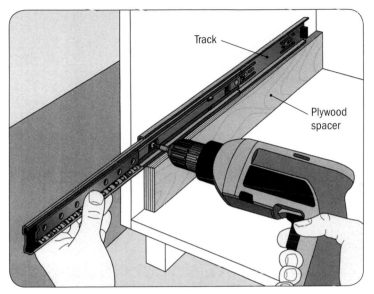

Track

Plywood spacer

Fasten Tracks

Position the tracks on the sides of the cabinet according to the desired spacing. For the lowest track, simply measure the offset of the drawer runner from the cabinet bottom, adding ¼ inch for clearance. Draw a line at this height. Hold the track against the cabinet side and center the predrilled screw holes over the line. For face frame cabinets, position the track so it is nearly flush with the front of the cabinet; for frameless cabinets, inset the track by the thickness of the false front stock. Fasten the track with screws. The higher tracks can be positioned by adding the drawer height specified on the cabinet story pole to the runner offset. Remember to measure to the center of the track. Repeat these steps for the other drawers.

SHELF SUPPORTS

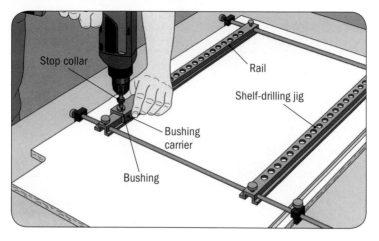

Stop collar

Rail

Shelf-drilling jig

Bushing carrier

Bushing

Adjustable shelving requires two parallel rows of holes to be drilled in the side panels of the cabinet case. The commercial jig shown above allows you to bore holes at 1-inch intervals and ensures the corresponding holes will be perfectly aligned. Set a side panel inside-face-up on a work surface and clamp the jig to the edges of the panel; the holes can be any distance from the panel edges, but about 2 inches in would be best for the panels shown. Fit your drill with a bit the same diameter as the sleeves and install a stop collar to mark the drilling depth equal to the sleeve length. Starting at either end of one of the jig's rails, place the appropriate bushing in the first hole of the bushing carrier. (The bushing keeps the bit perfectly square to the workpiece.) Holding the drill and carrier, bore the hole. Drill a series of evenly spaced holes along both rails. Remove the jig and repeat for the other side panel of the case, carefully positioning the jig so the holes will be aligned with those in the first panel.

SHELF DRILLING JIG

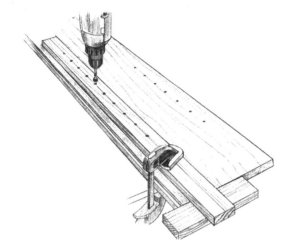

The T-shaped jig shown at right will allow you to bore a row of evenly spaced holes as accurately as a commercial jig. Make the jig from 1-by-3 stock, being careful to screw the fence and arm together at a perfect 90° angle. Mark a line down the center of the arm and bore holes along it at 2-inch intervals with the same bit you would use for threaded sleeves. To use the jig, clamp it to a side panel with the fence butted against either end of the panel and the marked centerline 2 inches in from its edge. Fit your drill bit with a stop collar, bore the holes, and reposition the jig for each new row.

CABINET DOORS

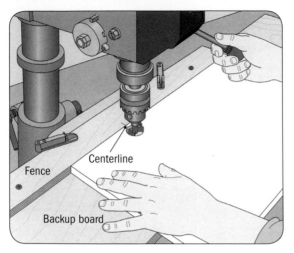

Centerline

Fence

Backup board

Hinge Holes

Drill the holes for European cup hinges with a commercial drilling jig and guide, or make your own jig by installing a plywood fence and backup board on your drill press. Fit the drill with a 35-millimeter Forstner bit, and screw the fence and backup board together as shown. Follow the hinge manufacturer's instructions regarding recommended boring depth and distance from the edge of the door; use a piece of scrap wood to properly position the jig. Clamp the jig to the drill press table, and mark the centerline of the hole on the fence. Next, mark the location of the hinges on the doors; depending on the size of the door you are working with, hinges can be installed anywhere from 3 to 6 inches from either end of the door; mark a similar centerline on the fence. Lay the door face down on the drill press table and butt it against the fence, aligning a hinge mark with the centerline. Hold the door steady and drill the hole. Slide the door along, line up the second hinge mark with the centerline, and drill the second hole.

CABINET DOORS *(continued)*

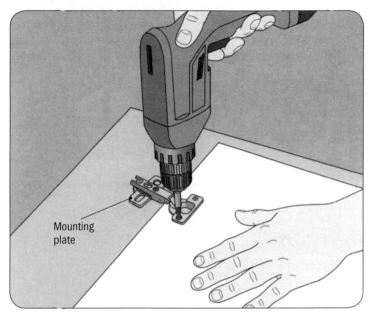

Mounting
plate

Installing the Hinge

Installing the hinges To work comfortably, place the door face down on a work surface. With the mounting plate attached to the hinge arm, fit the body of the hinge in the hole you drilled in step 1. Then, making sure that the hinge arm is perfectly perpendicular to the edge of the door, fasten the hinge in place with the screws provided by the manufacturer.

CABINET DOORS *(continued)*

Mounting Plate

With the mounting plate still attached to the hinge, align the door with the cabinet as shown, and extend the hinge arms to butt the mounting plate against the panel. Making sure that the adjustment screws on the mounting plate are in mid-position, mark a reference

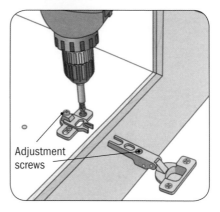

Adjustment screws

line, unscrew the mounting plate from the hinge arms, and fasten it to the cabinet side. This need not be overly precise; the hinge can easily be adjusted after installation.

Hanging the Door

Slide the hinge arms onto the mounting plate until they click into position, then screw them together. Close the door and check its position. Adjust the height, depth, or lateral position of the door by loosening or tightening the appropriate adjustment screws on the hinge arms and mounting plate.

CABINET DOORS *(continued)*

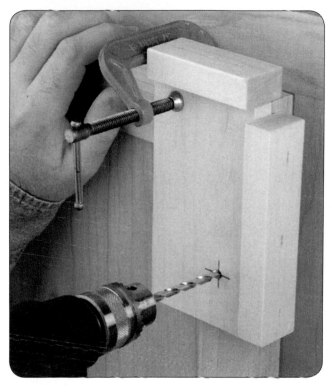

Locating Knobs

Locating doorknobs need not involve tedious measurement from door to door. The simple jig shown in the photo at right, made from a piece of plywood and two lips cut from solid stock, locates knobs in exactly the same spot on each door.

Index

INDEX

Back to *Basics*

Straight Talk for Today's *Woodworker*

ISBN 978-1-56523-463-5
$19.95 USD • 152 Pages

ISBN 978-1-56523-462-8
$19.95 USD • 200 Pages

Setting Up Your Workshop

Back to Basics

Woodworker's Guide to Joinery

Woodworker's Guide to Wood

Back to Basics

Woodworking Machines

Back to Basics

Constructing Kitchen Cabinets

Back to Basics

ISBN 978-1-56523-464-2
$19.95 USD
160 Pages

ISBN 978-1-56523-466-6
$19.95 USD • 144 Pages

ISBN 978-1-56523-465-9
$19.95 USD • 192 Pages

Get *Back to Basics* with the core information you need to succeed. This new series offers a clear road map of fundamental woodworking knowledge on sixteen essential topics. It explains what's important to know now and what can be left for later. Best of all, it's presented in the plain-spoken language you'd hear from a trusted friend or relative. The world's already complicated—your woodworking information shouldn't be.